Robbie Woods and His Merry Men

MICHAELA MORGAN

Illustrated by Doffy Weir

PACIFIC
L E A R N I N G

© 2001 Pacific Learning
© 1996 Written by **Michaela Morgan**
Illustrated by **Doffy Weir**
US Edit by **Rebecca Weber McEwen**

This Americanized Edition of *Robbie Woods and His Merry Men*,
originally published in English in 1996, is published by
arrangement with Oxford University Press.

05 04 03 02 01
10 9 8 7 6 5 4 3 2 1

Published by
Pacific Learning
P.O. Box 2723
Huntington Beach, CA 92647-0723
www.pacificlearning.com

ISBN: 1-59055-018-8
PL-7309

Contents

Chapter 1 4

Chapter 2 9

Chapter 3 12

Chapter 4 18

Chapter 5 24

Chapter 6 32

Chapter 1

I'm Robbie Woods.

I'm always the first one to crack a joke.

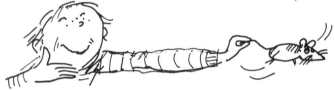

I'm always the first one to put away my work at the end of the day.

Somehow, though, I'm never the first one to be picked during sports or plays.

Big Bradley Tomlinson and Bossy Becky Sparrow always get to pick the teams for kickball.

"I choose Jack, Scott, Jordan, and Sam," Big Bradley says.

"I'll take Carly, Kylie, Katy, and Kaylee," Bossy Becky says.

6

It's the same with the school play.
In kindergarten, we did
Humpty Dumpty. I wasn't
Humpty Dumpty. I wasn't
one of the king's men.
I wasn't even a king's horse.
I was a brick in the wall.

In first grade, we
did *Cinderella*. I wasn't
the prince. I wasn't
a guest at the ball.
I wasn't even the
pumpkin.
I was a rock. I had
to stand there, looking
like a rock.

Then, in second grade, we did *The Pied Piper.*

No, I wasn't the Pied Piper.

I wasn't the mayor.

I wasn't one of the townsfolk, and I wasn't one of the children.

I was a rat.

This time I had a "speaking part." I had to say,

squeak squeak squeak squeak

If you ask me, it was more of a squeaking part than a speaking part.

Chapter 2

This year our play will be about Robin Hood and his Merry Men.

Our teacher, Ms. Chang, called everyone in the class together.

"What about his merry women?" Becky said. "It's sexist!"

"What about his miserable men?" Scott said. "It's miserablist!"

"What about just getting on with it?" Ms. Chang said. "Who would like to be Robin Hood?"

I shot my hand into the air.

I would!

"Robbie Woods would…" Ms. Chang said, writing my name on her list.

"Robbie Woods would. Robbie Woods would, would he…" Bradley began to chant.

I ignored him. "I know everything about Robin Hood," I explained.

"I know all the stories.
I've got all the books.
I've got a bow and arrow.
I've even got my own Robin Hood costume," I said.

"Hey, *I* want to be Robin Hood," Becky said.

"So do I," Bradley said.

So do I!

So do I!

So do I!

So do I!

So do I!

"I will give everyone a chance," Ms. Chang said. "These are the main roles."

Robin Hood
Maid Marian
Little John
Friar Tuck
Will Scarlet

Sheriff of
Nottingham
Allan a Dale
The Minstrel

"There are also parts for villagers, knights, and ladies... and of course we'll need lots and lots of trees to be the forest."

I can guess what I'm going to be.

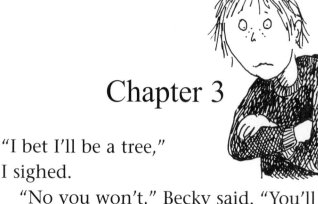

Chapter 3

"I bet I'll be a tree,"
I sighed.

"No you won't," Becky said. "You'll
be a little baby bush..."

"Or a teeny tiny twig," Bradley said.

"Quiet," Ms. Chang said.

*You can all try for a part.
Take a page of the script.
Practice it. Tryouts will be
Monday, and I'll decide who
will be best for each role.*

I took a copy of Robin Hood's part.

Robin Hood	Good morrow, lords and I. I am bold Robin Hood. I fight the foe with sword so bright and live in the greenwood. Forsooth I am a proud outlaw, a proud outlaw I be. I rob the rich to feed the poor and sleep under the greenwood tree.
Maid Marian	Good morrow, Robin Hood. What brings you here this day?
Friar Tuck	Ah, my lady, it is better to not ask this fellow such a question, or he will be called to tell you an untruth. Only smile upon him

There were lots of words.
Some were a little strange.

Forsooth?

Still, I was determined
to be Robin Hood.

13

I mean, if your name were Frankie Stein, you'd be interested in Frankenstein. Wouldn't you?

If your name were Richard King, you'd be interested in King Richard. Wouldn't you?

Well, my name, Robbie Woods, is just like Robin Hood. So it's only natural I'd take an interest in a hero with the same name (almost) as me. Isn't it?

I'm not the only one to notice how much I am like Robin Hood.

All my aunts and uncles give me Robin Hood presents.

I have Robin Hood teddy bears (I've had those since I was little).

I have Robin Hood jigsaw puzzles (and it's not easy doing a puzzle that is almost all green).

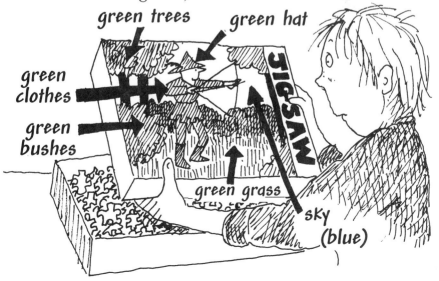

green trees

green hat

green clothes

green bushes

JIGSAW

green grass

sky (blue)

I have all the videos of all
the Robin Hood movies
and I have tapes of
Robin Hood songs.

I even made up a song.
I'd gallop around the playground
(when I was little) singing:

Robbie Woods, Robbie Woods
and his merry men,
Robbie Woods, Robbie Woods
here he comes again.
Feared by the bad,
Loved by the good,
Robbie Woods, Robbie
Woods, Robbie Woods.

There were other versions, mostly made up by Bradley. I didn't like those as much.

Robbie Woods, Robbie Woods
running around the school,
Robbie Woods, Robbie Woods
looking like a fool.
Feared by the sad,
Loved by the losers,
Robbie Woods, Robbie
Woods, Robbie Woods.

I don't care if Bradley teases me. I want to play the part of Robin Hood.

The trouble is – so does Bradley.

Chapter 4

Bradley is smart.
Very smart. Give him
words to learn and before
you can say

ABRACADABRA
or SHAZAM

or even YOU WHAT?

he's learned them.
I have to try a little harder, but I
took the script and decided I would
learn it by Monday.
I read the words
on the way home.

I said them loud and clear.

I practiced the actions.

At breakfast I practiced.

At bath time I practiced.

At bedtime I practiced.

It was hard. I kept forgetting things
and making mistakes but I didn't give up.

On Monday while everyone was out at recess I got my chance to try for the part.

"Take your time. Take a deep breath. Don't be nervous," Ms. Chang said.

I did it.

I spoke very loud and very clear.

I did some amazing acting, and I remembered every word.

I got the part.

"You really learned the part well,"
Ms. Chang said.

Pages
and pages
and pages
of it.

Chapter 5

Bradley got the part of Little John. He got that part because he's the biggest kid in class. He would have really preferred to be Robin Hood, though.

"I can't wait for our sword-fight scene," he said.

Then we'll see who the star is.

Becky would have loved to be Robin Hood, but she also would have been happy playing Little John. Instead she was cast as one of the ladies-in-waiting. She had to smile a lot and say, "Yes, my lady."

Jordan was the minstrel. He didn't want to be in the play at all but Ms. Chang insisted.

> You're perfect for the minstrel part. You're good at memorizing lines. You have a good, strong voice... and you're the only one who can play a guitar.

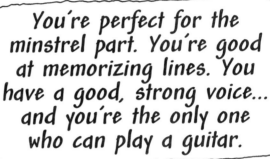

A minstrel is someone who tells stories and sings songs. The minstrel in our story was the narrator. He told the tale in song with a little strum of the guitar every now and then.

He had lots of words to learn – pages and pages of them.

Of course the biggest and best part was Robin Hood. Everybody wanted that part, but I'd won it.

A STAR AT LAST

"You'll never learn all that," Bradley said.  Why don't you give up now?

I was determined to be the best Robin Hood ever. I had the part of a hero, and a hero I would be.

I had three weeks to learn it. It was very hard.

I practiced in the park. My friends helped.

I practiced in the supermarket. My mom helped.

I practiced all the way to school. The crossing guard helped.

Here's a river to cross. Who stands in my way?

I'm Little John and I'm the boss. You can't cross here today.

Even Becky helped me. She was bored being a lady-in-waiting so she rehearsed with me. She played Little John's part and gave me hints on fighting.

I still got nervous, though, when everyone (especially Bradley) was watching. They seemed to be waiting for me to make mistakes.

I made plenty of them.

29

The more mistakes I made. The more nervous I got. The more nervous I got the more mistakes I made. The more nervous I got the more mistakes I made the more nervous

Jitters

I felt dizzy with worry.

Ms. Chang took me to one side.

"Robbie," she said. "Are you a little worried about the play?"

A little worried?

Oh no…

Sometimes I was hot and fevered.
Sometimes I was in a cold sweat.

SHIVERS *neebie*

I had knocking knees, cold feet, and
goose bumps as big as goose eggs.

WOBBLES **Shakes**

I had shaky hands, wobbly legs,
and butterflies as big as seagulls in
my stomach.

I wasn't a LITTLE worried…

I was TERRIFIED!!

I was still determined to
be Robin Hood, though.

Chapter 6

At home I did my best to practice, but since Grandpa came to live with us, we don't have very much spare room.

I got a great echo practicing in the bathroom, but no one was that happy about me practicing in there.

Then Grandpa said, "You can practice in my storage shed. That's the place for peace and quiet."

The shed is where Grandpa keeps all the piles of stuff he brought with him when Grandma died. He has boxes and boxes of this and that, and he's sure they'll come in useful.

He and Mom came down and cleared a space for me.

"If I move this box you can sit down here," Mom said to Grandpa. "Oh... look at that! It's your old banjo. You used to love playing that."

"Play me a song, Grandpa," I said.

He sighed. "It's not the same without your grandma," he said. "She used to love to hear me play."

"Well, *we'd* love to hear you play, wouldn't we?" Mom nudged me. She'd been trying to cheer up Grandpa for ages.

"You bet!" I said.

> In fact, could you help me with the minstrel scenes? You could sing his words and play the banjo.

"It would really help him," Mom agreed.

> Oh, all right...

Grandpa gave the banjo a half-hearted twang.

plink   Plonk

After half an hour there was no stopping him.

He was singing louder and louder, stomping his feet and playing faster and faster. He was really getting into the minstrel's part. He even made up a minstrel dance.

We practiced every day. He really cheered up and so did I. It made learning the words much easier and really funny.

I got an extra ticket for the play. I had a feeling that Grandpa would want to see it.

At school, rehearsals were going better. I was remembering my lines, but acting with Bradley was hard. The fighting-to-get-across-the-river scene was the worst. He would always shout his lines a little bit too loud.

He would slap my back a little bit too often.

He would always push a little bit too hard.

In the final dress rehearsal he really got carried away. He was waving his stick around in the air.

"Careful, Bradley," Ms. Chang said.

He was shouting louder and louder and pushing harder and harder until...

He lost his balance and fell off the bridge.

Ow! My ankle!

He had sprained his ankle.

"You won't be able to stand on that ankle for tonight's performance," Ms. Chang said.

Ouch!

"Will we have to cancel the play?" Becky asked.

Carly started to cry.

Kylie joined in.

Then Kaylee started.

They always do everything together. You'd think they were triplets.

WAAAH!

They wailed and sobbed and sobbed and wailed. Ms. Chang tried to make things better. "Nobody blames you, Bradley," she said, "so stop sulking. Carly and Company, will you stop that noise? I can't concentrate."

Can anybody else learn the part before tonight?

She looked at a group of boys.

| Scott shrugged. | Sam shook his head. | Jack shuffled his feet. |

Ms. Chang sighed. Everyone sighed. It was just not possible to learn the words and the actions in time.

Then Becky stood up.
"What about
me?" she said.

I've practiced the part with Robbie. I could do it really well. Carly could take my part as lady-in-waiting.

Carly stopped crying in mid-sniff.
"Could I?" she said.

Ms. Chang stopped frowning.

I sighed with relief.

Everyone cheered.

Carly and Co. burst into tears of joy.

"That only leaves one problem," said the secretary, coming in with a phone message.

Jordan the Minstrel has chicken pox.

"Oh no!" Bradley said.

"Oh no!" Becky said.

"OH NO!!!" everyone else said, except Carly and Co., who were crying fit to bust. Soon Becky had joined in and so had Jack. Even Bradley's nose was turning a little red.

sniff

Waaaah!

sob...

I didn't feel too happy myself.

After all I'd been through, I wouldn't be able to be Robin Hood.

Grandpa knows the words and he plays the banjo.

The banjo? I'm not sure a minstrel...

We called Grandpa anyway and he came to school.

| He showed how he knew all the words. | He showed how well he could play the banjo. |

He danced his crazy minstrel dance,
and everyone agreed he was fantastic.
He glowed with pride.
Ms. Chang sighed with relief
and I felt... like a hero.

Perfect!

In the performance that night he
was nearly perfect.

He just made one mistake. He kept
saying "Robbie Woods" instead of
"Robin Hood." I liked it.

46

Everyone clapped
and clapped
and clapped.

About the Author

I've written about fifty
stories for children.

I work at home and start
by making little, sloppy
notes on scraps of paper.
Then I type the story on
my computer. I put it in
my drawer and take it out
from time to time to make changes.
Each time I work on it, it gets a little bit better,
until eventually, I feel ready to send it to a
publisher.

Then, the publisher makes it into a book
like this, for you to read and enjoy.

Michaela Morgan